Miss Grace Green and the Clown Brothers

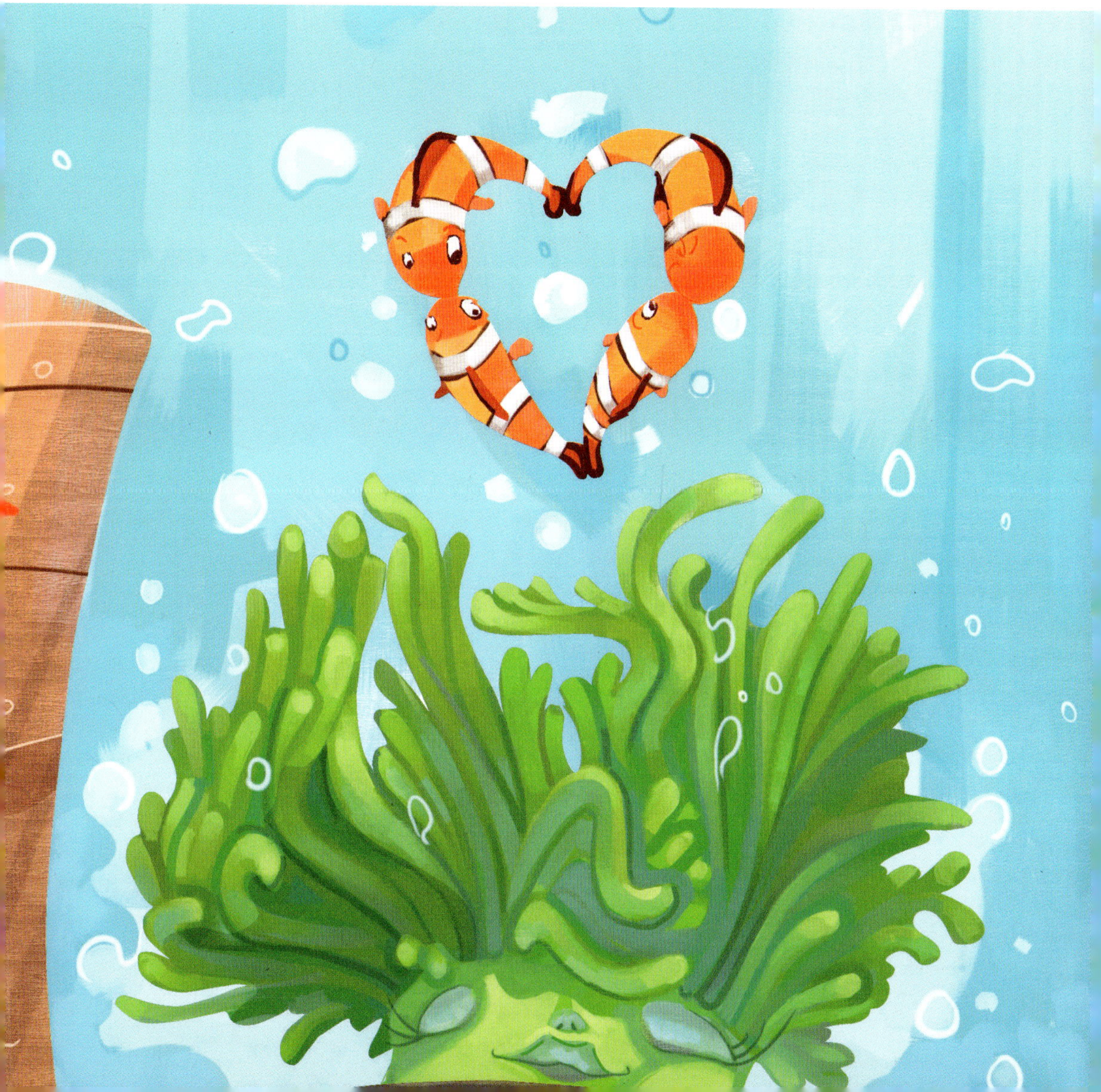

SPLISH! SPLASH!! SPLOSH!!!
In the deep blue sea there are three big fish.
One is yellow, one is purple, and one is black.
They're big, bad fish… and they're hungry!

The three big fish swim to a big white rock.
Behind the white rock there are four small fish.
They're orange and white.
They're happy. The sea is calm and they're playing.
PLISH, PLISH! PLISH, PLISH!

SPLISH! SPLASH!! SPLOSH!!!
The big fish are near the white rock.
'Oh no!' say the small fish. 'The big fish are coming!'
But the big, bad fish go away. They swim to a grey rock. They stop.

'Look! What is it?' says the yellow fish.
'Is it a fish? Is it a tree? Is it a fish-tree?'
says the purple fish.
'No... it's a flower!'
says the black fish.

'It's all green! It's an ugly flower!'
'It's a very ugly flower!'
'It's a horrible flower!'
'It's sleeping!' says the black fish, and he swims near the flower.
But the flower isn't sleeping. It's angry.

'I'm not ugly, I'm not horrible!'
It opens its eyes, it opens its arms and… WHAM!
'I've got you, stupid fish!'
'Help! I can't move!' says the black fish. 'You're an ugly, horrible flower! Help!'

Help! I can't move!

The yellow fish and the purple fish swim to the flower. They swim very fast. They've got an idea.
'I push his head, you pull his tail!' says the yellow fish.
'OK!' says the purple fish
'Ready, steady, go!'

'Push the head, pull the tail,
Push and pull, push and pull,
Push the head, pull the tail.'
POP!
The black fish is free!
The three fish swim away together.
SPLISH! SPLASH!! SPLOSH!!!

The deep blue sea is calm now.
The green flower isn't angry.
Its long arms dance in the water,
up and down and all around.
It looks like a dancer,
a beautiful dancer.

PLISH, PLISH! PLISH, PLISH!
The small fish are coming.
They swim slowly to the green flower. They stop.
'Look! She's wonderful!' they say. 'Wow! Is she a dancer? Is she a princess? Is she a sea-princess?'

Look! She's beautiful! Wow!

'Who are you?' they ask.
'I'm Grace Green,' says the flower.
'Hello, Miss Grace Green!' say the small fish.
'What a lot of beautiful green arms you've got!'
'Can you count how many arms I've got?' asks the green flower.

Who are you?

'Oh yes! One, two, three, four… and a lot more!'
The green flower smiles.
'You're funny,' she says. 'Who are you?'
'We're the Clown Brothers!'
'Sorry?' says Miss Grace Green.

I'm Grace Green.

'We're the Clown Brothers.'

'Oh, you're brothers!' says Miss Grace Green

'Yes! We're brothers. And we're clowns, too!'

Then they sing.

'We are clowns, we are brothers,

We are the champions, we are the best!'

'Sorry?' says Miss Grace Green.
'We are the champions,
We can make a square,
Swimming here and there!
We can make a circle,
We can make a heart,
Now it's time for us to start!'

PLISH, PLISH! PLISH, PLISH!
The Clown Brothers swim here and there.
They make a square, they make a circle.

They go very near the green flower and they make a wonderful heart.

Miss Grace Green smiles, and she touches the Clown Brothers with her long arms.

'You're the champions! You're very good champions!'

'Yes,' say the Clown Brothers, 'we're champions, but we're afraid.'

'Sorry?' says Miss Grace Green.

'We're afraid of the big, bad fish!'
'Oh, there aren't any big, bad fish here.
They are afraid of me!'
Look! My arms are long, my arms are strong.
My arms are strong for you and me.'

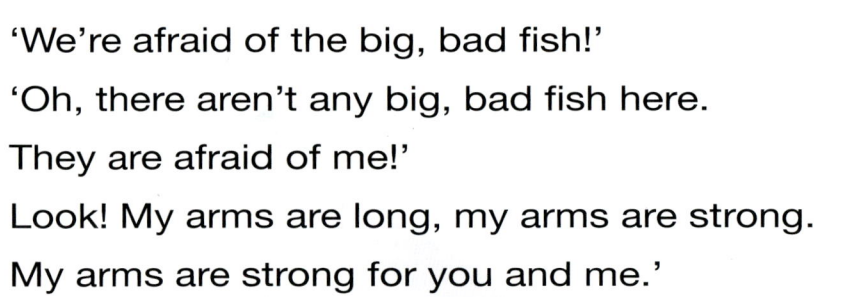

We're afraid of the big, bad fish!

'Really?' ask the Clown Brothers.
'Oh yes! You can stay here and play. The big bad fish are far away, and the sea is calm.'
The Clown Brothers stay.
They play their games.

Look!
My arms are long,
my arms are strong.

The clown fish swim up and down and all around the green flower.
They're happy, and Miss Grace Green is happy!
They're very good friends.
And when the big, bad fish come, they stay very near Miss Grace Green and sing together.

'Oh, big fish, can't you see?
We're the champions, we are strong!
We're the best in the deep blue sea!
We're all for one and one for all!'

Big and small fish

1 Read and circle 'yes' or 'no'.

Example: The three big fish are hungry.	(Yes)	No
1 They're big, bad fish.	Yes	No
2 They're clowns.	Yes	No

3 The four small fish are brothers.	Yes	No
4 They're champions.	Yes	No
5 They're small, bad fish.	Yes	No

Puzzle

2 Cut out ✂ and put in order.
Then turn them over and sing the song.

ACTIVITIES • 23

4. we're strong!	6. in the deep blue sea!
8. and one for all.	1. Oh big fish,
2. can't you see?	5. We're the best
7. We're all for one	3. We're the champions,

What is it?

3 Is it a big fish? Is it a small fish? Is it a flower? Colour the parts with the dots and discover what it is.

It's a _ _ _   _ _ _ _

Who is it?

4 Complete the drawing. Colour it.

Who is it? It's _ _ _ _   _ _ _ _ _ _   _ _ _ _ _

In the deep blue sea

5 Read the words in the sea and complete the balloons.

Can you draw…?

6 Use bubbles to draw. Can you draw…

…a big square?   …a small square?

…a circle?   …a heart?

…a big fish?   …a small fish?

…a big rock?   …a small rock?

ACTIVITIES • 27

A sea mobile

You need:

- a clothes hanger

- blue crepe paper

- white string

- scissors

- sticky tape

- felt-tip pens

7 How to make a sea mobile

① draw four clown fish

② colour them orange and white

③ cut the fish out

④ draw Miss Grace Green

⑤ colour her

⑥ cut her out

⑦ wrap the clothes hanger with the blue crepe paper

⑧ tie Miss Grace Green to the clothes hanger
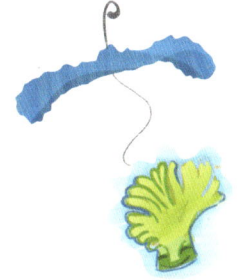

⑨ stick the clown fish to the 2 pieces of string

⑩ tie the clown fish to the clothes hanger

Picture Dictionary

dancer

princess

clown

brothers

champion

arms

eyes

head

heart

tail

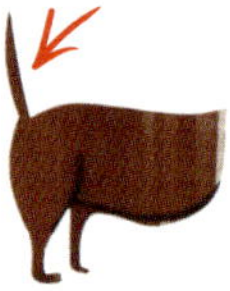

hungry

angry

strong

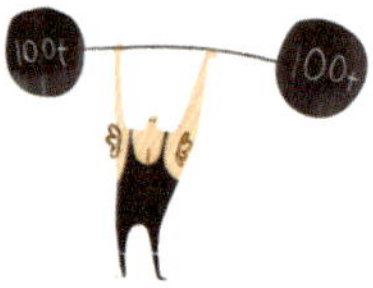

funny

afraid

big   small

long

beautiful ugly

up down

open

wonderful

around

move

horrible

push pull

good bad

swim

dance

look

count

slow 
fast

smile

come

here there

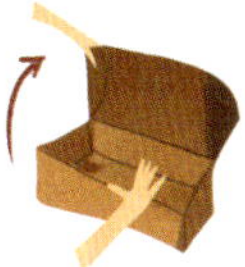

touch

go away

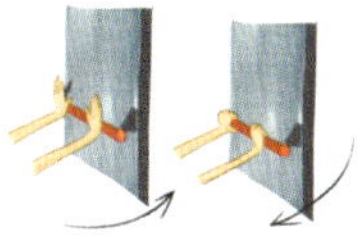

play

near far away

sleep

sing

Key

Activity 1:
1 Yes 2 No 3 Yes 4 Yes 5 No

Activity 3:
What is it? It's a big fish

Activity 4:
Who is it? It's Miss Grace Green

Activity 5:
In the deep blue sea
Clown fish: Look! She's wonderful! Wow!
Clown fish: Is she a dancer?
Clown fish: Is she a princess?
Clown fish: Who are you?
Grace Green: I'm Miss Grace Green

ACTIVITIES • 31

Editor: Robert Hill

Design and art direction: Nadia Maestri

Computer graphics: Carla Devoto

© 2011 Black Cat

First edition: January 2011

DEALINK, DEAFLIX are trademarks licensed by
De Agostini SpA

All rights reserved. No part of this book may be reproduced,
stored in a retrieval system, or transmitted,
in any form or by any means, electronic, mechanical,
photocopying, recording or otherwise, without the written
permission of the publisher.

We would be happy to receive your comments and
suggestions, and give you any other information concerning
our material.
info@blackcat-cideb.com
blackcat-cideb.com

Printed in Italy by Litoprint, Genoa